Egypt

CULTURES AND CELEBRATIONS

Greg Banks

PICTURE CREDITS
Cover: people gather at Tanta's Ahmed al-Badawi mosque during the Ahmed al-Badaw moulid (festival), Khaled el-Fiqi/EPA/AAP Image Library.

page 1 © Amro Maraghi/AFP/Getty Images; page 4 (bottom left) © Morton Beebe/Corbis/Tranz; page 4 (bottom right) © Hans Georg Roth/Corbis/Tranz; page 5 (top) © Jim Hollander/Reuters/ Stock Image Group; page 5 (bottom left) © Michael S. Yamashita/ Corbis/Tranz; page 5 (bottom right) © Richard T. Nowitz/Corbis/ Tranz; page 6, Corbis; page 8 © David Katzenstein/Corbis/Tranz; page 9 © Paul Stuart; Eye Ubiquitous/Corbis/Tranz; page 10, Photodisc; page 12 (top) © Christine Osborne/Corbis/Tranz; page 12 (bottom), Photodisc; page 14 © Neema Frederic/Corbis/ Tranz; page 15 © Barry Iverson/Time Life Pictures/Getty Images; page 16 © Amr Nabil/AP/Fotopress; page 21 © Neema Frederic/ Corbis/Tranz; page 22 (top) © John Lawrence/Stone/Getty Images; page 22 (bottom) © Neema Frederic/Corbis/Tranz; page 23 (top) © Mohamad al-Sehety/AP/Fotopress; page 23 (bottom) © Amr Nabil/AP/Fotopress; page 24 (top) © Amr Nabil/ AFP/AAP Image Library; page 24 (bottom) © Marwan Naamani/ AFP/AAP Image Library; page 25 (top) © Jeffrey L. Rotman/Corbis/ Tranz; page 25 (bottom) © Marwan Naamani/AFP; page 26 (top) © Amr Nabil/AFP; page 26 (bottom) © AFP; page 29 (top), Photodisc; page 29 (bottom), Digital Vision.

Produced through the worldwide resources of the National Geographic Society, John M. Fahey, Jr., President and Chief Executive Officer; Gilbert M. Grosvenor, Chairman of the Board; Nina D. Hoffman, Executive Vice President and President, Books and Education Publishing Group.

PREPARED BY NATIONAL GEOGRAPHIC SCHOOL PUBLISHING
Ericka Markman, Senior Vice President and President, Children's Books and Education Publishing Group; Steve Mico, Vice President and Editorial Director; Marianne Hiland, Executive Editor; Richard Easby, Editorial Manager; Jim Hiscott, Design Manager; Kristin Hanneman, Illustrations Manager; Matt Wascavage, Manager of Publishing Services; Sean Philpotts, Production Manager.

EDITORIAL MANAGEMENT
Morrison BookWorks, LLC

PROGRAM CONSULTANTS
Dr. Shirley V. Dickson, Program Director, Literacy, Education Commission of the States; Margit E. McGuire, Ph.D., Professor of Teacher Education and Social Studies, Seattle University.

CONTENT REVIEWER
Dr. Hesham Elnakib, Director, Egyptian Press and Information Office, Washington, D.C.

National Geographic Theme Sets program developed by Macmillan Education Australia, Pty Limited.

Published by the National Geographic Society
1145 17th Street, N.W.
Washington, D.C. 20036-4688

ISBN: 0-7922-4769-8

Product 42009

Printed in Hong Kong.

2008 2007 2006 2005
1 2 3 4 5 6 7 8 9 10 11 12 13 14 15

Contents

Cultures and Celebrations

Culture is the way people in one group live that makes them different from other groups. Culture is made up of many different things. These include traditions, language, dress, ceremonies, and other ways of life that a group of people share. Celebrations are also an important part of culture. By looking at countries such as Mexico, Italy, Japan, and Egypt, you can see how cultural practices bring people together.

 ## Key Concepts ....

1. Every society has a way of life that people share. This way of life makes up its culture.

2. Culture and celebrations help create a sense of national identity among people.

3. Some parts of culture change, but modern and traditional activities can exist side by side.

Four Different Cultures

Mexico

Mexican culture includes Spanish and Mexican Indian customs.

Italy

Regional customs and the Roman Catholic religion are important in Italian culture.

In this book you will learn about the customs and celebrations that make up the culture of Egypt.

Japan

Modern city life and ancient customs and values combine in the culture of Japan.

Egypt

The Islamic religion and a strong sense of history are important in Egypt's culture.

The Culture of Egypt

Picture yourself in the busy Egyptian city of Cairo, in the rich valley of the Nile River, or in the vast Sahara Desert. Do you see some people dressed in modern clothes and others in older-style garments? Look at the **mosques** where followers of the Islamic faith worship. Look at the pyramids that the **pharaohs** built thousands of years ago. They stand very close to modern buildings. Listen to the people. Some are speaking Arabic, the national language. Others are speaking French, English, and local languages.

Egypt's history goes back about 7,000 years. The ancient Egyptians built many great cities, temples, and tombs. The most famous structures are the pyramids of Giza. These pyramids were built as tombs for the pharaohs.

Most of the land in Egypt is desert. Its hot, dry climate has helped to preserve many of Egypt's ancient structures. One giant structure, the Great Sphinx, has the head of a man and the body of a lion.

The Great Sphinx

Egypt Today

Egypt is a country in northeastern Africa. It has a proud, rich history. Egyptians regard their country as the **intellectual** center of the Middle East. Although Egypt is in Africa, its religion and ways of life are closely related to those of Middle Eastern countries.

Over time, many foreign powers have influenced the Egyptian way of life. For example, people from the Middle East brought the religion of Christianity to Egypt more than 1,900 years ago. The religion of Islam was introduced 1,400 years ago. It was brought to Egypt by the Arab people of the Middle East. Today, most Egyptians follow Islam. Their religion influences how Egyptians live their lives.

Look at the map. It shows you where Egypt is located.

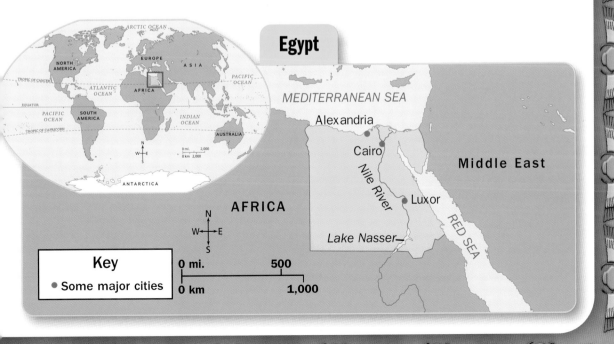

Key Concept 1 Every society has a way of life that people share. This way of life makes up its culture.

Societies and Their Cultures

Culture affects the way people live. Some parts of culture are obvious to people outside the culture. How people dress, what they eat, family life, and religious practices are some obvious examples of culture. Other aspects of culture are not so obvious. These include what people believe and what they value.

culture
the language, dress, values, celebrations, and other ways of life that a group of people share

This woman's traditional clothing is a part of her culture that is easy to see.

Egyptian Food In the past, Egyptian farmers grew crops of lentils, barley, wheat, and beans in the Nile River valley. The river supplied plenty of water to farmers. The river also improved the soil. When the Nile flooded, it deposited rich silt on the land. The silt made the soil very fertile. Farmers still grow food in this fertile area.

Egyptians make many types of bread, including a flat bread called pita bread. Pita bread is popular throughout the Middle East. It is often eaten with hummus or tahini. Hummus is made mostly from chickpeas. Tahini is made from ground sesame seeds.

Pita bread is often served with shish kebabs. Shish kebabs are made of meat and sometimes vegetables cooked on a skewer. The meat is usually lamb or chicken. A shish kebab can be eaten straight off the skewer. It can also be stuffed into pita bread.

Shish kebabs are made and sold on the streets in Egypt.

Egyptian Beliefs and Values

To ancient Egyptians, religion was very important. They believed in many gods. They thought these gods had control over different things. For example, they believed that the goddess Renenutet was responsible for a good harvest. The people performed **rituals** and made offerings, which they believed would please their gods.

Today, most Egyptians are Muslims. Muslims follow the religion of Islam. Practicing the beliefs of Islam is important to many Egyptians. Islam gives people guidance for how to dress, what to eat, and how to live. Muslims are expected to turn toward the holy city of Mecca in Saudi Arabia for prayers five times a day. Mecca is the most holy city for all Muslims. Islam also requires its followers to fast for one month a year. They do this in a month called Ramadan. During Ramadan, Muslims do not eat anything between dawn and dusk. Muslims are also expected to travel to Mecca once in their lives. This journey is called a *hajj*.

Many Egyptians place great value on the family. Egyptian families often include grandparents, aunts, uncles, and cousins all living in the same house together.

Muslim people worship in buildings called mosques.

Key Concept 2 Culture and celebrations help create a sense of national identity among people.

Culture and National Identity

Certain things bring Egyptians together as a people. Some of these are objects, such as the Egyptian flag or famous artworks. Language and various **celebrations** also bring people together. All these things help to give the Egyptian people a **national identity**.

> **national identity**
> feelings of belonging shared by the people of a country

Flag Look at the Egyptian flag. Each of its bold stripes has a special meaning to the culture and national identity of Egypt's people. The red stripe represents the Egyptian people's struggle for freedom. The white stripe signifies new beginnings and a bright future. The black stripe is a reminder of how Egypt suffered when the country was occupied by other countries.

In the middle of the white stripe is the eagle of Saladin. Saladin was a Muslim leader who lived during the 1100s. The eagle is clutching a panel that has the country's name in Arabic. The flag is a **symbol** of Egypt's independence as a country.

Art Egypt has a long tradition of artistic expression that goes back to ancient times. Ancient Egyptians believed in life after death, and artwork in the tombs was very important. It included carved masks and paintings portraying scenes of the afterlife. Temples were covered with bright images of daily life. Ancient Egyptian paintings had a strict style. People's heads were shown from the side, or in profile, and their bodies were shown from the front. This style did not change much for thousands of years.

An ancient Egyptian painting

Sculpture and **architecture** were important parts of ancient Egyptian art. This can be seen in the statues, pyramids, and temples that still stand today. These ancient statues and buildings are part of Egypt's national identity.

In Egypt today, Islamic art often features **geometric** designs and intricate patterns. Calligraphy, an elaborate writing style, is also used.

An ancient Egyptian mask

Music Egyptians have enjoyed music for thousands of years. Ancient Egyptians used music in recreation and religious ceremonies. The art in tombs and temples shows people dancing, clapping their hands, and playing musical instruments. Instruments used long ago are still played today. These instruments include harps, flutes, pipes, horns, drums, and cymbals. Egyptian music has its own distinctive sound. It has spread across the world and has influenced music in other cultures.

One of Egypt's popular singers in the 1950s and 1960s was named Um Kulthum. She combined Eastern and Western themes in her songs and promoted Arab music. Another famous Egyptian singer is Amr Diab. He won the World Music Award in 1998. Amr Diab's music was popular in Europe and in the United States. Music helps give Egyptians a strong national identity.

Language The official language of Egypt is Arabic. People in different parts of Egypt speak in different **dialects**. This means they use different sounds and words.

There are 28 symbols in the Arabic alphabet, which is written from right to left. Written Arabic spread to Egypt through the teachings of Islam. The sacred book of Islam, called the Koran, is written in Arabic. Some English words that have derived from Arabic include *magazine* and *algebra*.

جمهورية مصر العربية

This Arabic script reads "Arab Republic of Egypt."

Celebrations

Many Egyptian celebrations are Islamic celebrations. *Id al-Fitr* is the festival that marks the end of Ramadan, the fasting month. During this festival, people give presents to their families. They also wear special clothes and eat special food. Muslim Egyptians also celebrate their religion in other ways. They make a **pilgrimage** to Mecca, and they commemorate the prophet Mohammed's birthday.

There are many public festivals, or *moulids*, held throughout Egypt. A moulid is an annual celebration to honor the special saint of a city or village. Moulids include groups of people called *Mawalidiya*, who travel from moulid to moulid. The Mawalidiya provide carousels, swings, cafés, and stalls for selling candy, clothes, and toys. Mawalidiya also put up tents for Muslims called Sufis. The Sufis perform chants and dress in brightly colored costumes.

Family members attend festivals and ceremonies together.

Changing Culture

Over time, some aspects of **traditional** Egyptian cultural practices have changed. They have changed because of the influences of the modern world. Egyptian culture has been strongly influenced by outside cultures.

> traditional
> handed down
> through time

Dress In ancient Egypt, people wore clothes made of linen. Most workers wore simple loincloths. Wealthy men wore rectangles of fabric tied around their waists like kilts. Women wore long, close-fitting dresses with one or two straps over the shoulders.

Today, many people in rural areas dress in traditional Arab styles. Men wear loose pants and long shirts. Women wear long, flowing gowns. These loose-fitting clothes keep people cool in the hot climate. Some people who live in cities wear clothing styles that are also popular around the world. These styles include jeans and business suits.

Some Muslim Egyptians wear traditional Islamic clothes. Men wear long gowns and **skullcaps**. Many men grow beards. Women wear robes and a veil. They keep their hair, ears, and arms covered.

A woman in business dress

Games   Ancient Egyptians played many sports. These sports are often depicted in ancient drawings and **inscriptions**. They include sports similar to hockey, handball, gymnastics, javelin throwing, fishing, wrestling, and weight lifting.

One of the most popular sports in Egypt today is soccer. Egyptians are very enthusiastic about their soccer teams. When the two most popular teams in the Egyptian national league play each other, millions of fans watch the game. Fans also support the Egyptian national team. Many people in Egypt play soccer as well.

Egypt's Walid Salah falls during a soccer match against Morocco.

Customs   One Egyptian custom is to refuse when someone offers something or gives you an invitation. If the offer is sincere, not just made out of politeness, it will be repeated. To show good manners in Egypt, a person waits for the second offer before accepting. If you are offering an Egyptian something, you might need to ask twice if you really want the person to accept.

Egyptians use gestures to communicate. They shake their heads to show they do not understand. Egyptians raise their eyebrows and lift their heads up and back to say no. Or they might also say, "tsk, tsk." Holding your right hand over your heart means, "No, thank you," when you are offered something you don't want.

Think About the Key Concepts

Think about what you read. Think about the photographs and illustrations. Use these to answer the questions. Share what you think with others.

1. Name at least two values that are part of the culture of the people in this book.

2. How have the flag, art, and language helped give these people a national identity?

3. Tell about two cultural celebrations in this country.

4. Discuss at least two examples of how modern parts of culture and traditional parts of culture exist side by side.

Comparison Chart

A chart allows you to find specific facts quickly and easily. You can learn new ideas without having to read many words. Charts use words and a box-like layout to present ideas.

There are different kinds of charts.
This chart of countries and their cultures is a **comparison chart**. It compares information about different countries.

How to Read a Comparison Chart

1. **Read the title.**
   The title tells you the subject, or what the chart is about.

2. **Read the column headings.**
   Columns go from top to bottom. The heading at the top of each column tells you what kind of information is in the column.

3. **Read the row headings.**
   Rows go from side to side. The headings in the left column name the countries you will get information about as you read across the rows.

4. **Connect the information as you read.**
   Read across each row to find information about a subject. Read down each column to compare information.

Countries and Their Cultures

Country	Population	Land Area Square kilometers	Capital City	Main Religion	Flag
Mexico	104,959,594	1,923,040	Mexico City	Roman Catholicism	
Italy	38,057,477	294,020	Rome	Roman Catholicism	
Japan	127,333,002	374,744	Tokyo	Shinto and Buddhism	
Egypt	76,117,421	995,450	Cairo	Islam	

What Are the Facts?

Write sentences telling all the facts you learned about one of the countries in the chart. Share with a classmate who chose a different country. What is similar about the countries? What is different?

Photo Essay

A **photo essay** is a group of photographs and captions that tell about an event or place.

Photo essays are usually printed in magazines or newspapers. Their purpose is to show images connected to the event or place that they are about. Photo essays also try to help people understand the feelings or emotions behind the event or place.

Id Al-Fitr
An Egyptian Celebration

The **title** tells the topic of the photo essay.

More than 90 percent of the population of Egypt is Muslim. Many Egyptian celebrations are based on events in the Islamic calendar. Id al-Fitr is a festival at the end of the fasting month of Ramadan. The name Id al-Fitr means "festival of breaking the fast." The actual date of Ramadan varies, depending on the cycles of the moon.

The **introduction** gives an overview of the topic.

Photographs tell the story of the topic in pictures.

Thousands of people are gathered here in Cairo to pray together. Their prayers mark the end of Ramadan, the month of fasting. During Ramadan, Muslims pray to remember those who are poor and in need.

Captions add information and help explain the pictures.

This is the Muhammad Ali mosque in Cairo. Egyptian mosques, or Muslim houses of worship, are always very busy on Fridays. Friday is the traditional day of prayer for Muslims. Mosques are even busier during Ramadan and Id al-Fitr.

These people are praying together at the time of Id al-Fitr. After prayer, they will greet their neighbors, friends, and relatives. They give gifts to each other and to charity. Traditionally, children receive clothing to be worn during the celebrations.

Egyptian women prepare traditional sweets for the Islamic feast of Id al-Fitr. The feast lasts for three days following the fasting month of Ramadan.

Many people journey to Cairo from rural areas to join their relatives in celebration. Trains and buses all around the country are crowded during this time.

This boy looks over a crowd of worshippers bending in the first prayers of Id al-Fitr. After the prayers are finished, celebrations will begin.

Music is an important part of the Id al-Fitr celebrations. This man is a Sufi Muslim. Sufis have many traditions, including ritual dances, songs, and prayers. Sufis also give blessings to the crowds that gather to celebrate the end of Ramadan.

These Bedouin people are preparing lamb for their Id al-Fitr feast. Bedouins are animal herders who live in the desert. They live in tents and move from place to place. Many Bedouins have given up their traditional lifestyle. They have become farmers and live in houses.

Street vendors gather outside the mosques to sell balloons and toys. Parents buy presents for their children to mark the end of the month of fasting. This man has toy soccer balls for sale.

These girls are enjoying a bumper car ride at an Id al-Fitr festival.

At the end of Ramadan, Muslims pray, give gifts, and have feasts. This woman prepares traditional cookies for the celebration. Traditions like these are an important way for people to celebrate their culture together.

Apply the Key Concepts

Key Concept 1 Every society has a way of life that people share. This way of life makes up its culture.

Activity Make a chart with two columns. Think about your American culture or the culture of your heritage. In the first column, list some parts of your culture that are easy to see. In the second column, list some parts of your culture that are not easy to see.

Easy to See	Hard to See
dress	

Key Concept 2 Culture and celebrations help create a sense of national identity among people.

Activity Draw a picture of the Egyptian flag and a picture of the American flag. Write a caption under each flag explaining what the colors and symbols of the flags mean. You may need to do some research about the American flag. Then write about the similarities and differences between the American and Egyptian flags.

The flag symbolizes . . .

Key Concept 3 Some parts of culture change, but modern and traditional activities can exist side by side.

Activity List some traditional parts of Egyptian culture. Next to each one, write whether it is still practiced today. Describe any modern practices that exist alongside it or have replaced it.

1. Traditional dress	1. Still worn but modern clothing is also worn.

Create Your Own Photo Essay

Egypt's culture includes many practices, traditions, and celebrations. You have read about some of them. Now it's time to think about your culture. Get ready to make your own photo essay about your culture. You may choose your American culture or the culture of your heritage.

1. Study the Model

Look back at the photo essay on pages 21–26. Think about how the photos and captions work together to tell a story. How do the photos show the actions and feelings of the people? How do the captions help you understand the photos? You'll want to think about these things as you plan your own essay.

Creating a Photo Essay

◆ Write a title that tells the topic of the photo essay.

◆ Choose photographs that show different things about the topic.

◆ Organize the photographs into a story.

◆ Write an introduction that summarizes the topic.

◆ Write captions that help tell the story.

2. Choose and Plan Your Topic

Look through books and websites for photos that show your culture. The topic of your photo essay should be an event, place, or group of people in your culture. Try to find several different photos that relate to one event, place, or group of people. Make sure that you can find enough photos related to the topic. Then read about your topic. Make notes on what you find.

3. Organize Your Materials

Photocopy photos you want to use from books and magazines, or print photos from the Internet. Look for photos that show people and their actions. Choose the photos that tell your story best. Your photos should cover different parts of your topic, and some should show people's feelings. Write down facts about each photo. You can use these to write captions.

Many Americans have picnics on the Fourth of July.

4. Make a Draft

Think about the best order for the photos in your photo essay. Which one introduces the topic best? Lay out the photos in an order that makes them easy to understand. Write one caption for each photo. The captions should help tell the story. Then write an introduction. The introduction should summarize the topic and get people interested in your photo essay.

5. Revise and Edit

Look at the photos and read your text. Correct any mistakes. Do the photos tell a story? Do the captions and introduction add information and help explain the photos? Paste the photos onto sheets of paper in the order you've chosen. Put your title and introduction on a separate page. Copy your captions carefully under each photo.

Create Your Own Photo Exhibition

Now you can share your work. An exhibition is a display that you might see in a gallery or a museum. Follow the steps below to make a photo exhibition.

How to Make a Photo Exhibition

1. **Make each photo essay into a poster.**
   Paste the pages of the photo essay on poster board.

2. **Decide on an arrangement for the photo essays.**
   You might want to group essays with similar subjects. For example, photo essays about celebrations could go on one wall.

3. **Display the photo essays.**
   Make sure they are at a good height. People should be able to look at the photos without looking too far up or down.

4. **Choose a name for the exhibition.**
   The name should describe the theme of the exhibition.

5. **Make a catalogue for the exhibition.**
   A catalogue tells visitors to an exhibition about the items on display. Write a description for each photo essay. Label the descriptions with the titles of the photo essays, and type them in the order in which they have been arranged on the walls. Make copies for the people who will visit the exhibition.

6. **Have a grand opening for your exhibition.**
   You could invite parents or students from another class. Give each guest a catalogue, and let them look at the exhibition.

Glossary

architecture – the design and planning of buildings

celebrations – special activities done to show that a holiday or other event is important to a group of people

culture – the language, dress, values, celebrations, and other ways of life that a group of people share

dialects – regional ways of speaking a language, including different ways of saying words or using some different words

geometric – made with straight lines and simple shapes such as triangles, squares, and circles

inscriptions – words carved into an object such as a stone or a coin

intellectual – relating to the mind, learning, or knowledge

mosques – buildings where Muslims practice their religion

national identity – feelings of belonging shared by the people of a country

pharaohs – rulers in ancient Egypt

pilgrimage – a journey made for religious reasons

rituals – meaningful ceremonies done in specific, traditional ways

sculpture – the art of carving or shaping something out of stone, clay, metal, or other materials

skullcaps – small, tight-fitting hats with no brims

symbol – a thing that represents something else

traditional – handed down through time

Index